£7.99

we ♥ love you...
TINIE TEMPAH
An Unauthorised 2012 Annual

Written by Rebecca Bowden
Designed by Chris Dalrymple

PBR

A Pillar Box Red Publication

© 2011. Published by Pillar Box Red Publishing Ltd.

This is an independent publication. It is completely unofficial and unauthorised and, as such, has no connection with the artist or artists featured, or with any organisation or individual connected in any way whatsoever with the artist or artists featured.

Any quotes within this publication which are attributed to the celebrity, or celebrities, featured have been sourced from other publications, or from the internet, and, as such, are a matter of public record. They have not been given directly to the author by the celebrity, or celebrities, themselves.

Whilst every effort has been made to ensure the accuracy of information within this publication, the publisher shall have no liability to any person or entity with respect to any inaccuracy, misleading information, loss or damage caused directly or indirectly by the information contained within this book.

The views expressed are solely those of the author and do not reflect the opinions of Pillar Box Red Publishing Ltd. All rights reserved.

Photography © Shutterstock.com and BigPictures.co.uk except for:
Pages 2-3: Rowan Miles/EMPICS Entertainment
Page 32: Ian West/PA Wire/Press Association Images
Page 33: Yui Mok/PA Wire/Press Association Images
Page 63: Suzan/Suzan/EMPICS Entertainment

ISBN: 978-1-907823-19-0

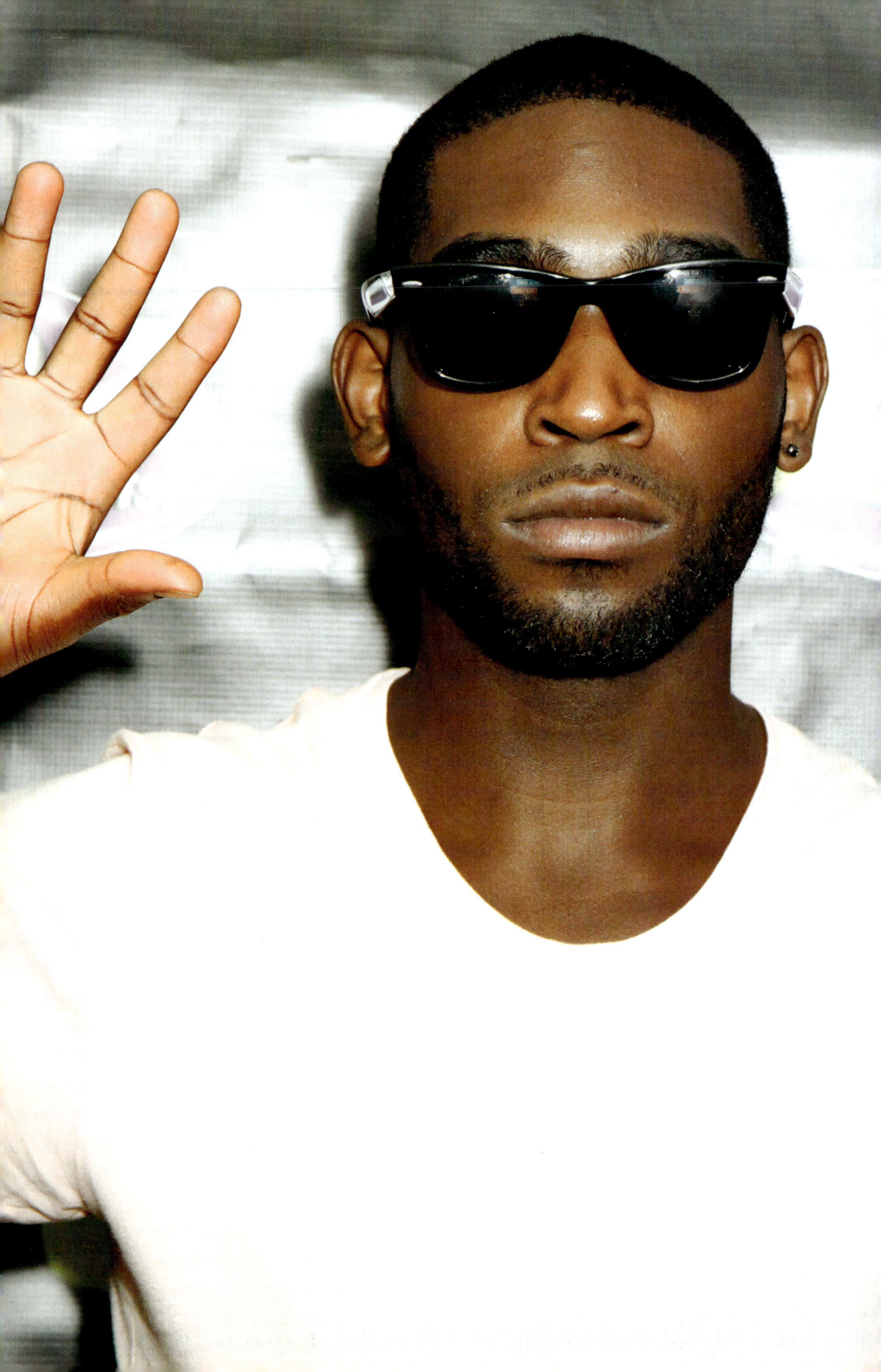

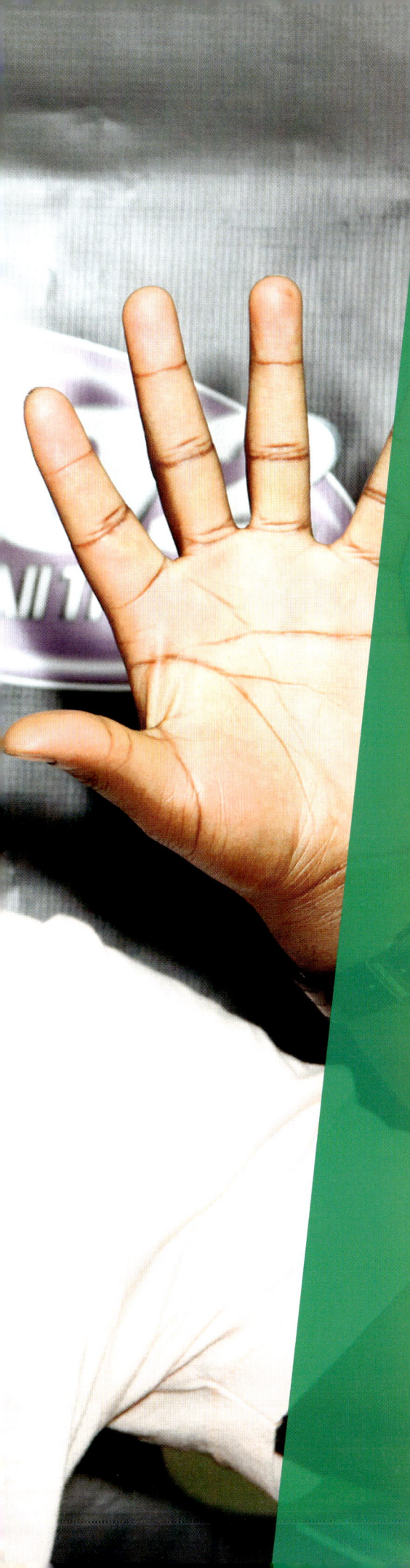

CONTENTS

Page 08	We Love You Tinie Because...
Page 12	History – Rise to Fame
Page 16	Tinie Quotes
Page 18	Spot The Difference
Page 19	Wordsearch
Page 21	Discography
Page 22	Tinie Loves...
Page 24	Live on stage
Page 27	Crossword
Page 28	What's Tinie's Sign?
Page 29	On This Day
Page 32	Awards
Page 34	Charitable Man!
Page 36	Famous Friends
Page 38	Tinie Gossip
Page 42	Tinie's Inspirations
Page 44	So You Wanna Be A Star?
Page 47	Colouring in
Page 48	Collaborations
Page 50	Lyrics Quiz
Page 51	Colouring in
Page 52	Look to the Future
Page 56	Tinie Fashion Focus!
Page 58	A-Z of Tinie
Page 61	Quiz Answers
Page 62	Where's Tinie?

we ♥ you...

TINIE TEMPAH

Because...

You're Gorgeous!

You are determined to succeed!

You inspire us with your lyrics!

You have your own sense of style and know how to rock it!

You love your fans and never take them for granted!

You remember your roots and where you came from!

You don't take yourself too seriously!

Your live shows are amazing and you really connect with your fans from the stage!

You have achieved so much for such a young artist!

You have worked with some of the coolest musicians worldwide!

You keep releasing successful tracks that make us want to dance!

You are an individual!

You are a great performer!

TINIE TEMPAH FACT FILE

Name: Tinie Tempah
Birth Name: Patrick Chukwuemeka Okogwu (Jr.)
D.O.B: 07.11.1988
From: Plumstead, South London
Famous For: Being one of the UK's most talented new Rap/Hip Hop stars.
Height: 5ft 9 inches
Marital Status: Single
Star Sign: Scorpio
Likes: Fashion, Fast Cars, Music
Dislikes: Being Stereotyped, Mustard, Creased Clothes
Most Recent Album: Disc-Overy
First Number One Single: Pass Out
Celebrity BFFs: Kylie Minogue, Mr Hudson, Chipmunk.

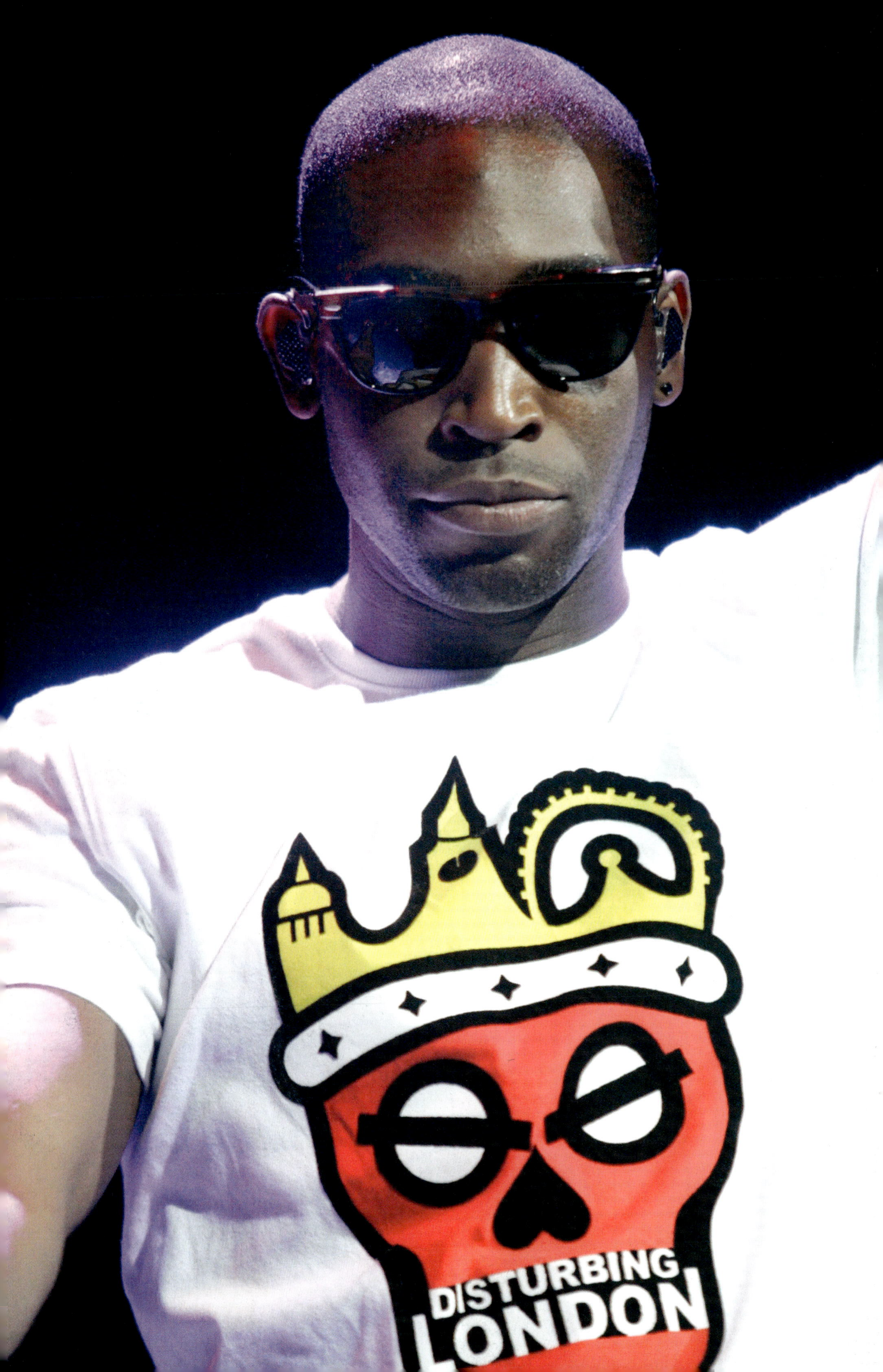
DISTURBING
LONDON

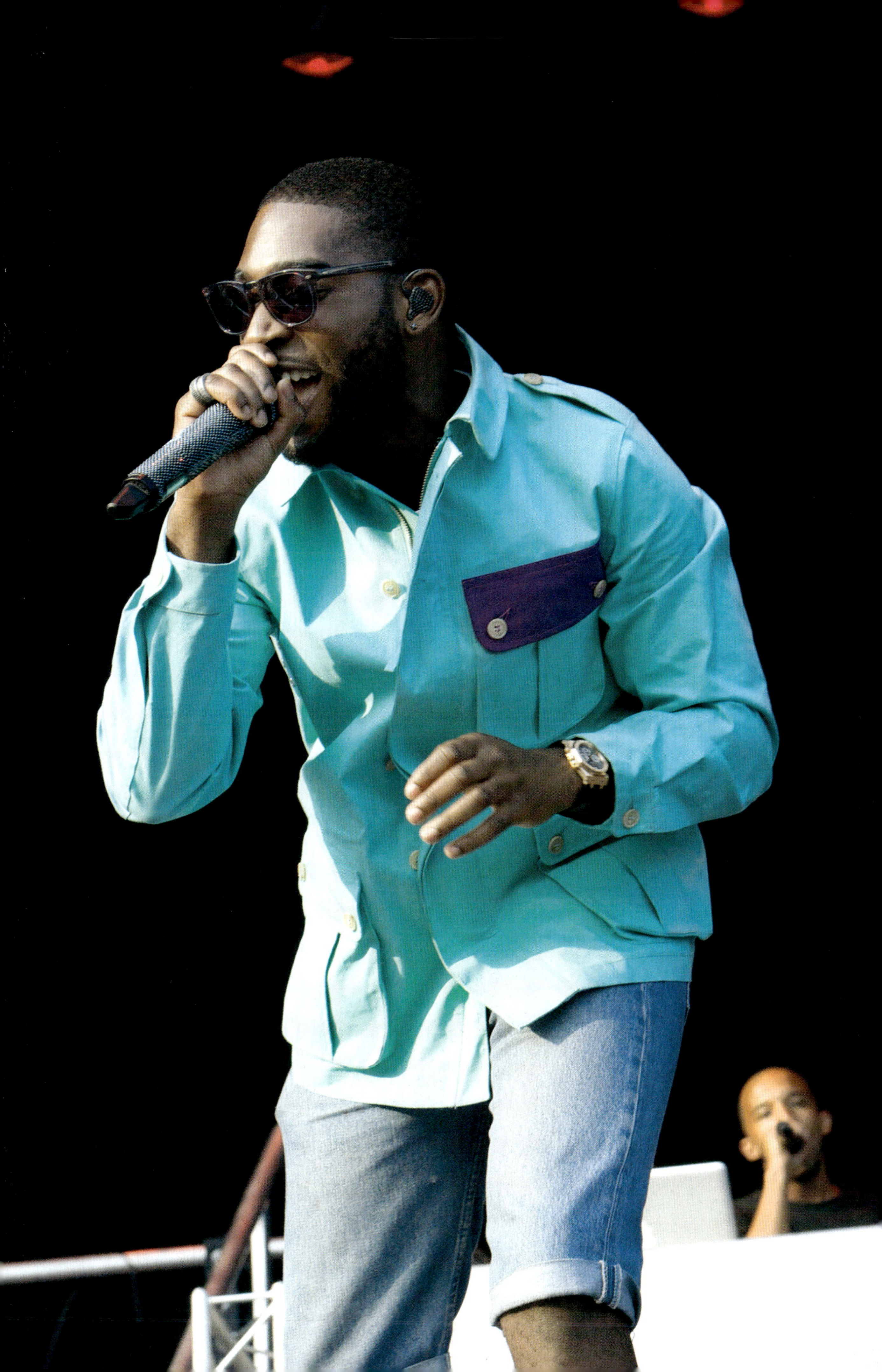

TINIE TEMPAH
RISE TO FAME

Born in South London on 7th November 1988, this is where Tinie Tempah (real name Patrick Chukwuemeka Okogwu Jr.) began the first crucial steps in his rise to fame.

Every star has to begin somewhere and for Tinie that time came in 2006 when his music began getting good air play on the UK music TV channels, with his song *Tears* proving to be especially popular with the public.

Although things were already going well and he was definitely on the showbiz radar, Tinie Tempah's world was about to change forever when his big musical break came courtesy of Sony and their PSP game 'Wipeout Pure', which featured one of his songs *Listen to the Vibe* along with Yazmin & DJ Ironik.

After a promotional European tour it was at the 2009 Wireless Festival that Tinie was spotted by a talent scout, music consultant Jade Richardson. She was so impressed with his talent and already ever-developing fan base that she immediately called Parlophone Records president, Miles Leonard, who signed Tinie, taking him one step closer to super stardom! He later went on to tour with fellow Brit hip hop rapper Chipmunk in 2010. The two of them are still close friends today.

In late February 2010 Tinie launched his major label debut single *Pass Out* which was a massive hit, entering the singles chart straight in at number one and becoming the soundtrack of the summer for many music lovers. This sent Tinie catapulting into star status. In little to no time *Pass Out* had received over 4 million views on YouTube, confirming just how much support the Tinie Tempah fans were prepared to give him!

Following up his success and proving that he was no one hit wonder, Tinie released his second single *Frisky* on 6th June 2010 and it entered the UK singles chart at number two. More good times quickly followed on 25th June 2010 at Glastonbury Festival when Tinie Tempah played to a packed crowd on the Pyramid Stage, something incredibly life changing for such a young rapper.

When singing sensation Rihanna came to the UK for a 10 date tour, Tinie was the supporting act for four shows, giving him maximum exposure to millions of fans. He also supported Mr Hudson, performed at Radio 1's Big Weekend in Bangor, the Summertime Ball at Wembley Stadium, T4 On The Beach and the Wireless Festival in London's Hyde Park, and both days of the V Festival on 21st and 22nd August 2010. Keeping Tinie a very busy boy indeed!

On 19th September 2010 Tinie was ready to release his third single. *Written in the Stars* was produced by Swedish powerhouse Ishi and featured vocals of Boston newcomer Eric Turner. The song details Tinie's past, present and future ambitions. Talking about the song's positive message within the lyrics, he says 'I'm trying to live the dream and other people can do the same if they put their mind to it. That's what the song is about. You can do everything I've done, if you're determined and driven enough.'

October 2010 was another busy month for Tinie who was still gaining in popularity and experience, working with more influential musicians and releasing his fourth single, *Miami 2 Ibiza*, on 1st October 2010 and then his eagerly awaited debut album *Disc-Overy* on 4th October 2010. Critics and fans raved about the album and it continues to do well in the charts.

His first ever UK tour kicked off in style on 11th October 2010 supported by American hip-hop band Chiddy Bang, and was a huge success.

Since then Tinie has released more singles including *Invincible* (featuring Kelly Rowland), *Wonderman* (featuring Ellie Goulding), *Simply Unstoppable* (Yes Remix) (featuring Travis Barker and Katie Taylor) and *Till I'm Gone* (featuring Wiz Khalifa) to name but a few. He is still very much at the peak of his career and 2011 has already been kind to this talented hip-hop mega star with another tour on the way and an appearance at the 2011 Glastonbury Festival, once again on the prestigious Pyramid Stage.

Tinie has confirmed that he is currently writing his second album, the expected release date for this is 2012 although nothing has been officially confirmed. So keep a look out for it as this will most definitely be one album that you don't want to miss!

TINIE TEMPAH
RISE TO FAME

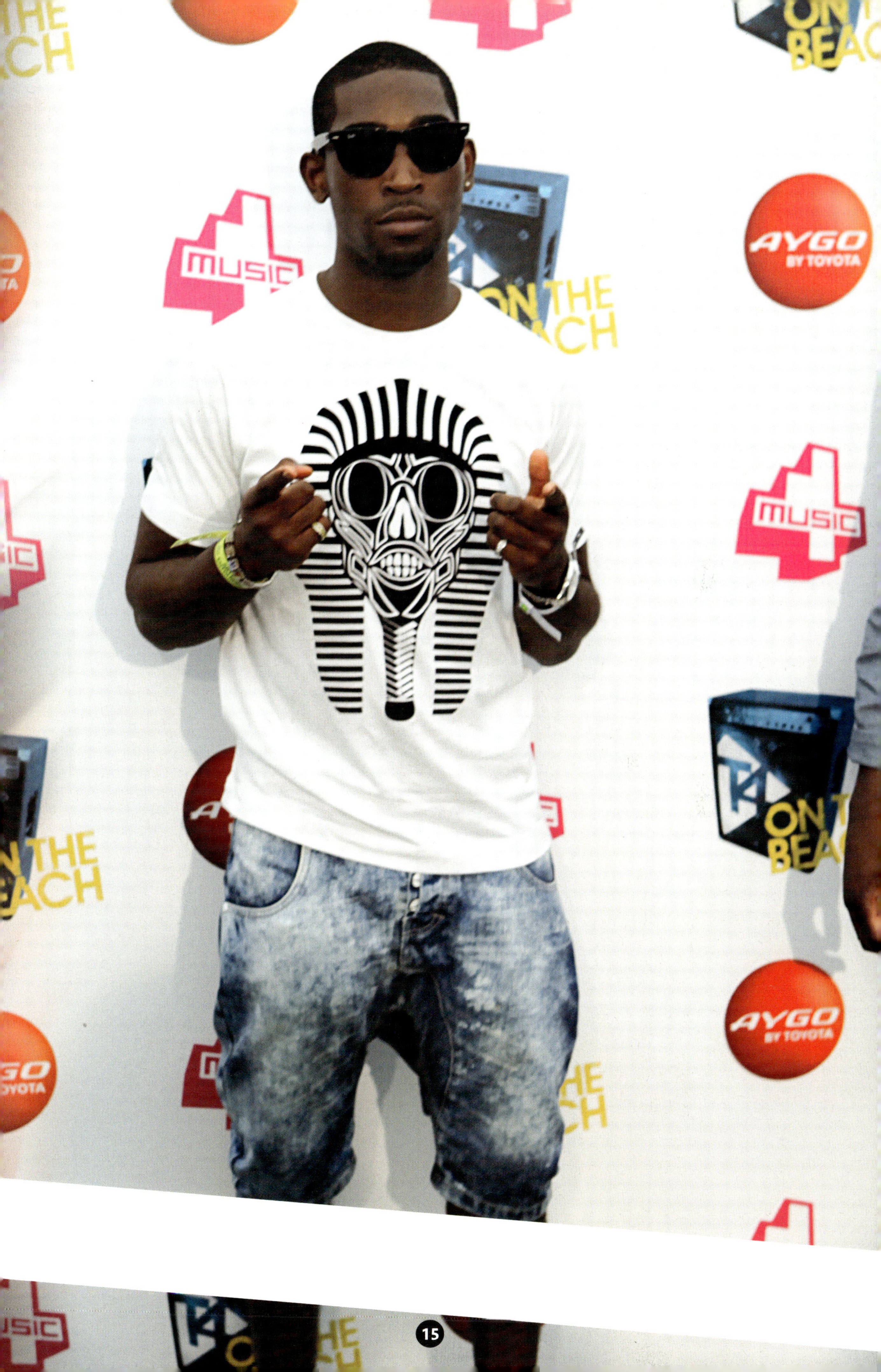
MUSIC
ON THE BEACH
AYGO
BY TOYOTA

TINIE QUOTES

We all know that Tinie Tempah is the man in the spotlight right now. So wherever he goes and whatever he does, people want to chat with him and to find out what he thinks. Take a look at some of these cool Tinie Tempah quotes and lyric snippets!

Talking to 'More!' magazine about his celebrity crushes Tinie said:

'Rihanna is incredible. Frankie from The Saturdays is hot, Jade from Sugababes, Alexandra Burke, Pixie Lott.'

From *Written in the Stars* on the DISC-OVERY album:

'I used to be the kid that no-one cared about, it's like you have to keep screamin' till they hear you out.'

Speaking on 'Twitter' about his album sales:

'Woop Woop DISC-OVERY currently #10 on iTunes US.. Please support and buy your copy if u haven't already...LOVE!'

Speaking on his official blog about the first time he heard his track *Pass Out* on the radio Tinie says:

'I still have vivid dreams about the first day I heard *Pass Out* on daytime radio… It was such a revolutionary moment for me, I listened to it objectively, as a fan…I turned the radio up and then down again and then off and then on and it felt right, it felt like something amazing was on the verge of happening and it did, not just for me but for black music and music with an underground origin. To this day, a year on *Pass Out* is still in the Top 75 making it the joint 20th longest runner of all time.'

When speaking to 'Buzzine' about his time on tour in the US:

'I think L.A. is an incredible place… in the space of four days, I bumped into Quentin Tarantino, Lil' Wayne, Lionel Richie… That would be impossible in England. Four days and I saw all of those people, and I very much like it. It's very much "you and me are here now; let's get up, let's go, let's make it happen." And New York is very much the same as well.'

Speaking to The Guardian Newspaper in February 2011, Tinie says:

'I'm from an era where we have an iPod and that has a button called 'Shuffle' which mixes up all your favourite artists. All these different artists come up and you never change it. I've kind of adapted that with what I do musically. I don't believe in separating the genres. There's no reason I shouldn't do Glastonbury. Whether it's rap or rock 'n' roll, if it's a good song, it's undeniable.'

After picking up an award for Best Contemporary Song for *Pass Out* at the Ivor Novello Awards:

'I honestly came here not thinking I was going to win because this is as big as it gets and this is the one that people respect the most and I'm really happy now to be a part of its history.'

Speaking to 'Choice FM' about an upcoming O2 Arena show:

'It's going to be really exciting; this is a real big thing. I've dreamed about doing the O2 Arena, I can't wait for the opportunity so it's going to be insane.'

Speaking to NME.com about his much talked about upcoming second album, Tinie says:

'The second album is well under way, it's sounding amazing. I've been in the studio with Pharrell quite a lot recently and we've been working on a few things and obviously Stargate. I'm really happy, I just want to take my time and make sure it's right. The first album has done so many amazing things, I want to make sure the second one is twice as good.'

SPOT THE DIFFERENCE
Can you spot the 9 differences?

WORDSEARCH

Find the words in the grid. Words can go horizontally, vertically and diagonally in all eight directions

```
Q L F O B O M D C R H D T G K
V V F I D P Z D T A X T C K R
L P L N F N R R P L G Y A Y E
P N P V N D H M K M J Z H N P
N R M I F M E I G Y L H G A P
R N Y N T T Z Z P D K H U M A
L V W C E U K R R H S H O R R
N B W I R Q O A R I O J R E D
W Y N B D N W S L J Z P H D L
T I Z L C A H Y S L L R T N L
T Q T E T N T T E A H R K O K
L M K I K S V T D P P F A W N
Q B R M Y M G N Y M T T E P H
M B P V K O X N M N Y T R K Z
Y F R I S K Y R X Y R T B L D
```

BREAKTHROUGH ACT
BRIT AWARD
FRISKY
HIP HOP
INVINCIBLE
LET GO
MOBO
PASS OUT
RAPPER
STYLISH
TINIE TEMPAH
WONDERMAN

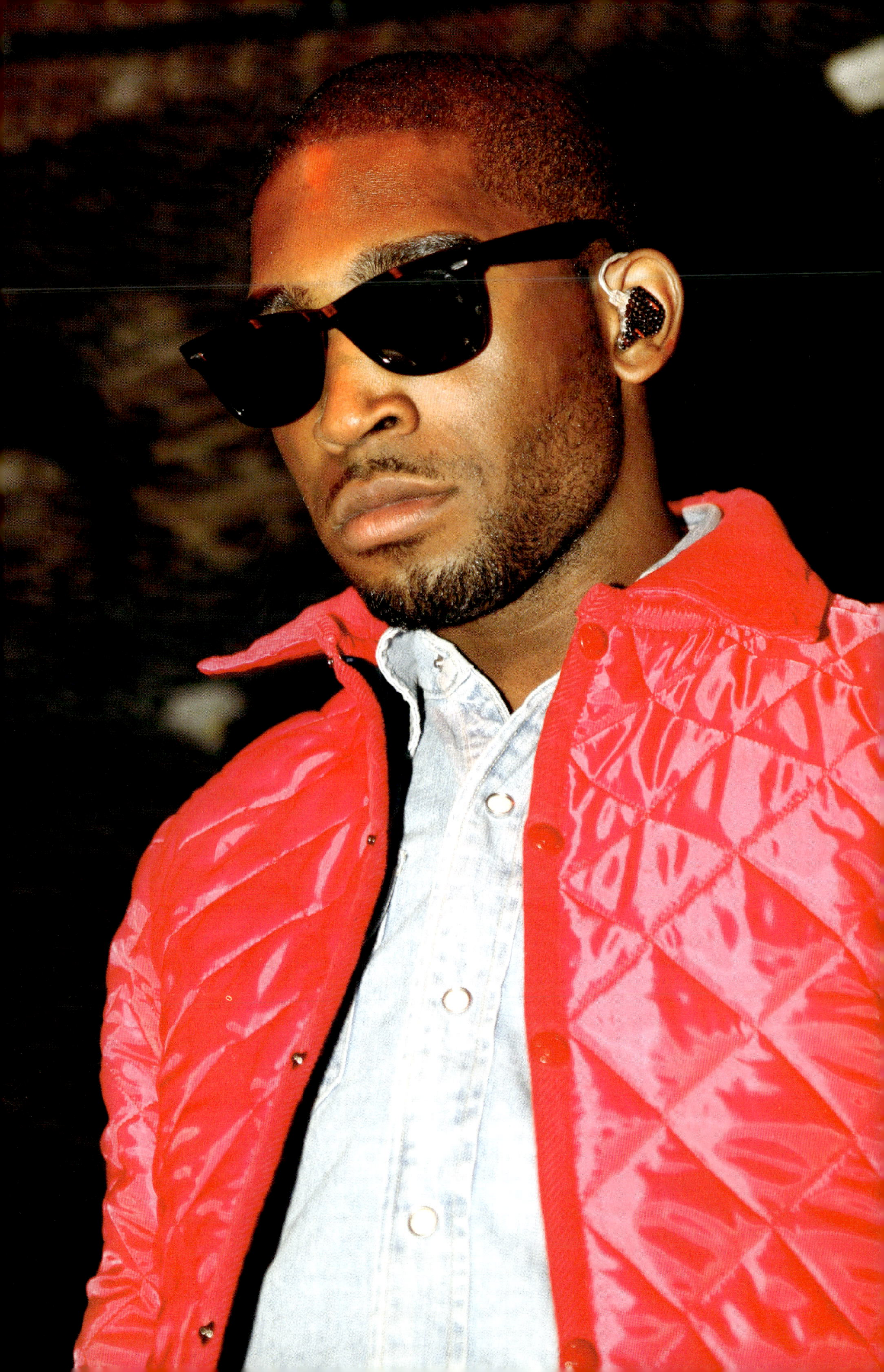

DISCOGRAPHY

ALBUMS

2007
Hood Economics - Room 147:
The 80 Minute Course - DL Records

2010
Disc-Overy - Parlophone

SINGLES & EPS

2007
Tinie Tempah vs. Maresa MacBeth -
Put The Guns & Knives Down

2008
Tears

2010
Pass Out
Tinie Tempah ft. Eric Turner - Written In The Stars
Swedish House Mafia vs. Tinie Tempah -
Miami 2 Ibiza (The Mixes)
Tinie Tempah ft. Labrinth - Frisky
Wrongtom vs. Tinie Tempah - Pass Out

2011
Tinie Tempah ft. Ellie Goulding - Wonderman
Tinie Tempah ft. Kelly Rowland - Invincible

TINIE LOVES

Tinie Tempah is a great musician and a huge rising British talent. We already know how much WE love Tinie, but what are the things that Tinie Tempah loves?

His Ray-Ban Glasses - Tinie loves his trade mark glasses and sunglasses and he is rarely seen without them on; even when he's inside! There's no question about it, he certainly knows how to work that superstar charm!

Music - Tinie has a great appreciation for music, especially in the rap and hip-hop genre and is always blogging and talking about his favourite tracks of the week and the artists that he loves to listen to himself!

His Friends - Tinie has a good mix of celebrity friends and those who he grew up with. He seems like the type of guy who always makes time for his friends when they need him!

His Family - Tinie is very family orientated, he is close to his family and often refers to them in his song lyrics.

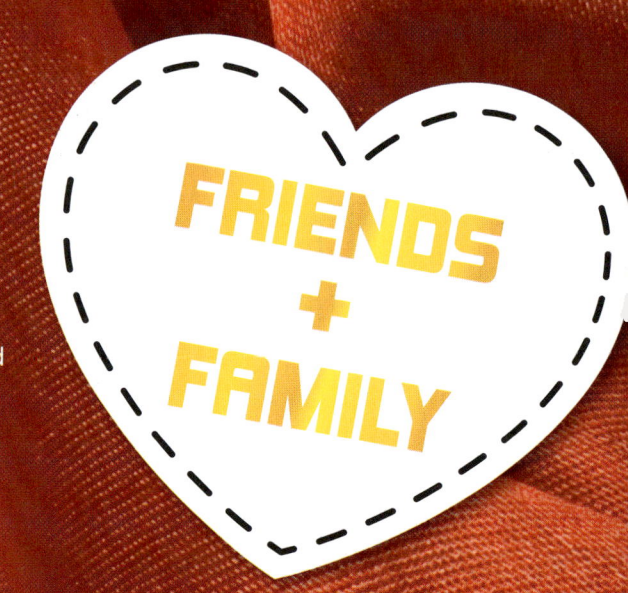

FRIENDS + FAMILY

Fashion - Tinie spends a lot of time looking at fashion and picking out the items that fit his own unique style. He loves to look good and takes great pride in his appearance.

His Fans - Tinie Tempah is always raving about his fans and just how important they are to him. He never forgets their love and support and shows kindness and gratitude to them whenever he has the opportunity.

Cars - Tinie has a great love of cars, especially the fast ones! He enjoys looking at their design and specifications and regularly posts images and videos of them online.

Working with Well-Known Musicians - Tinie knows how to pick the best musicians to collaborate with in his work. He loves working with other artists that he admires and always has a good selection of celebrities, stars and well known personalities wanting to work with him on his latest single.

Trainers – Tinie Tempah has always had a love of shoes and trainers! He loves Nike and Converse and other well known brands and just can't resist the latest styles and brands!

His Blog - If you visit the official Tinie Tempah website online you will see that Tinie is keeping up with the latest internet trends and even has his very own blog. He loves to connect to fans through this and give them a sneak peek into his lifestyle.

Being Online – Tinie Tempah loves being online and using all of the social networking channels to stay in touch with his fans. He has an official twitter account and a blog and enjoys posting updates, images and information on the things that he finds interesting. This makes him even more accessible and in tune with his fans!

LIVE ON STAGE

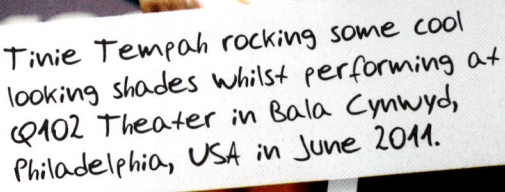

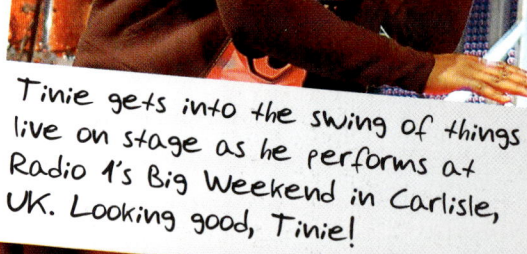

Tinie Tempah rocking some cool looking shades whilst performing at Q102 Theater in Bala Cynwyd, Philadelphia, USA in June 2011.

Tinie gets into the swing of things live on stage as he performs at Radio 1's Big Weekend in Carlisle, UK. Looking good, Tinie!

Feeling the heat! Tinie Tempah wows the crowds as he performs in concert at the BankAtlantic Center in Sunrise, Florida, USA.

Tinie Tempah looking cool in Khaki clothing on the first night of his 2011 sold out tour at Manchester Apollo, UK.

Raise your hands in the air for Tinie Tempah as he performs live at Jalouse nightclub in London, UK to a packed crowd.

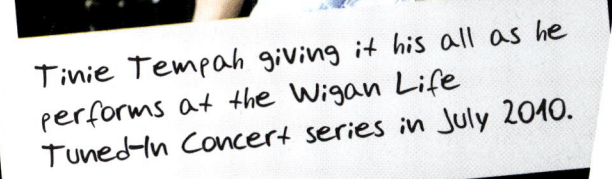

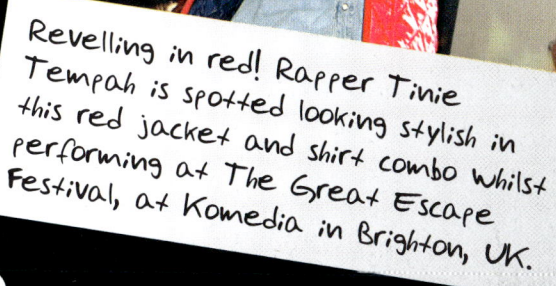

Who's that guy?! Oh yeah, it's Tinie Tempah performing live at Blackberry presents MTV's Brand New For 2011, KOKO, London, UK. Looking every bit the super star!

Tinie rocks the crowds on Day 2 of V Festival at Weston Park, Shropshire, in August 2010.

It might be 2010 The Big Chill Festival, but Tinie is hotting things up live on stage at Eastnor Castle, Hertfordshire, UK.

Tinie Tempah giving it his all as he performs at the Wigan Life Tuned-In Concert series in July 2010.

Revelling in red! Rapper Tinie Tempah is spotted looking stylish in this red jacket and shirt combo whilst performing at The Great Escape Festival, at Komedia in Brighton, UK.

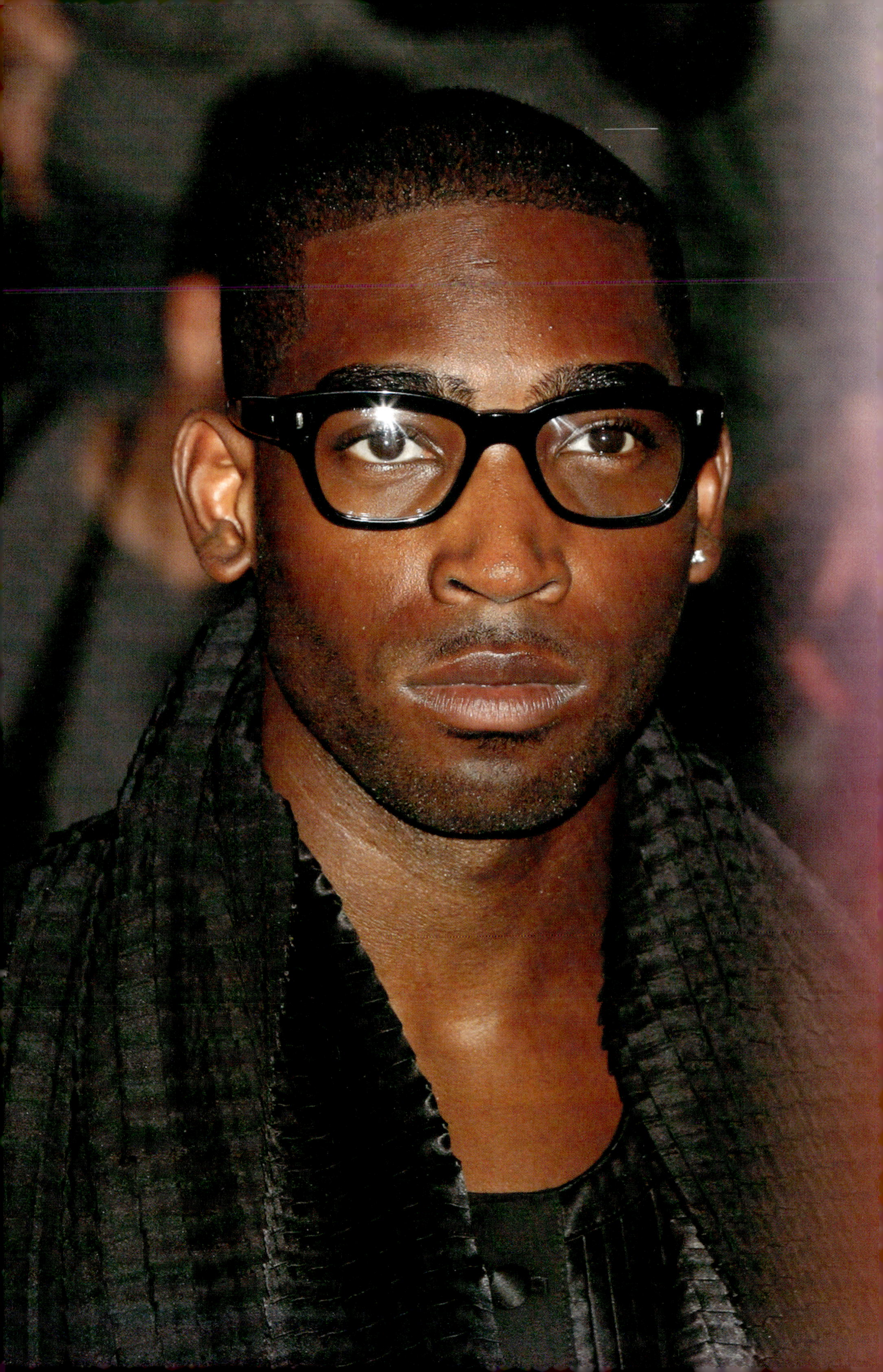

CROSSWORD

ACROSS

3   What is Tinie Tempah's real first name? (7)

5   Tinie keeps his clothes at his ____'s house (4)

6   _____ London - Tinie's record label (10)

10 This supernova artist has toured with Tinie - Mr _____ (6)

13 Married to Beyonce Knowles and has toured with Tinie (3, 1)

14 "Oh written in the stars a _____ miles away…" (7)

15 Tinie's home city (6)

17 Tinie's album (9)

18 Ellie Goulding collaborated on this track (9)

19 This IT girl booked a private performance with Tinie on Ibiza (5, 6)

DOWN

1   Tinie performed at Radio 1's Big _____ 2010 (7)

2   _____ in the Stars - a hit for Tinie and Eric Turner (7)

4   _____ House Mafia created a dance floor anthem with Tinie (7)

5   Heidi and _____ eat your heart out (7)

7   Tinie performed with this rap legend at Glastonbury 2010 (5, 4)

8   Artist who was featured on *Frisky* (8)

9   The *Umbrella* star who toured with Tinie (7)

11 Gorillaz front man who performed with Tinie Tempah on the Jonathan Ross Show (5, 6)

12 Artist who supported Tinie on his first UK tour (6, 4)

16 Tinie's first Number One (4, 3)

WHAT'S TINIE'S SIGN?

He was born on 7th November 1988 so that makes Tinie Tempah's star sign Scorpio! What do we know about Scorpio's and who are they compatible with? Let's take a look...

Quick Facts

Symbol: Scorpion **Stone:** Topaz **Element:** Water
Most Compatibile With: Other water signs like fellow Scorpios, Pisces or Cancer.
Ruling Planet: Pluto **Colours:** Dark Red, Black, Maroon

Scorpios like Tinie Tempah are strong willed, determined and creative. They are usually thought of as a real force to be reckoned with and are one of the most intense and powerful signs in the zodiac.

Scorpios are persistent, determined to succeed and have great depth. They tend to be full of energy and are really fun to be around. They enjoy to be challenged and don't like to lose. Those with a Scorpio star sign are also said to be incredibly loyal and protective friends.

Other Famous Scorpios

Tinie is in good company with his star sign! There are many other celebrities and mega stars out there who share it; you may just be surprised at how many movies you have seen with a famous Scorpio in them. Here are just a few...

Leonardo DiCaprio

Anne Hathaway

Ryan Gosling

Gerard Butler

Owen Wilson

Avril Lavigne

Rachel McAdams

On This Day

Tinie Tempah was born on 7th November 1988 but what other important events have taken place on 7th November throughout the years? Check out these other exciting and interesting events that happened on Tinie Tempah's Birthday in other years.

November 7th 1893 — Women in Colorado gain the right to vote.

November 7th 1865 — The London Gazette, the oldest surviving journal, is founded.

November 7th 1990 — Mary Robinson is elected as first female President of the Republic of Ireland.

November 7th 1990 — "Those Were The Days" opens at Edison Theater NYC for 126 performances.

November 7th 1998 — US Senator John Glenn, the United States' oldest astronaut at age 77, returns to Earth aboard the space shuttle Discovery after a nine-day mission.

November 7th 1980 — Famous actor Steve McQueen dies in Juarez, Mexico, at the age of 50.

November 7th 1951 — Singer-actor Frank Sinatra marries actress Ava Gardner.

November 7th 1492 — The Ensisheim Meteorite, the oldest meteorite with a known date of impact, strikes the earth around noon in a wheat field outside the village of Ensisheim, Alsace, France.

November 7th 1872 — The ship Mary Celeste sails from New York, and was eventually found deserted.

November 7th 1907 — Jesús García saves the entire town of Nacozari de Garcia, Sonora in Mexico by driving a burning train full of dynamite six kilometres away before it can explode.

So, you see November the 7th really was a busy day in various years all the way through history!

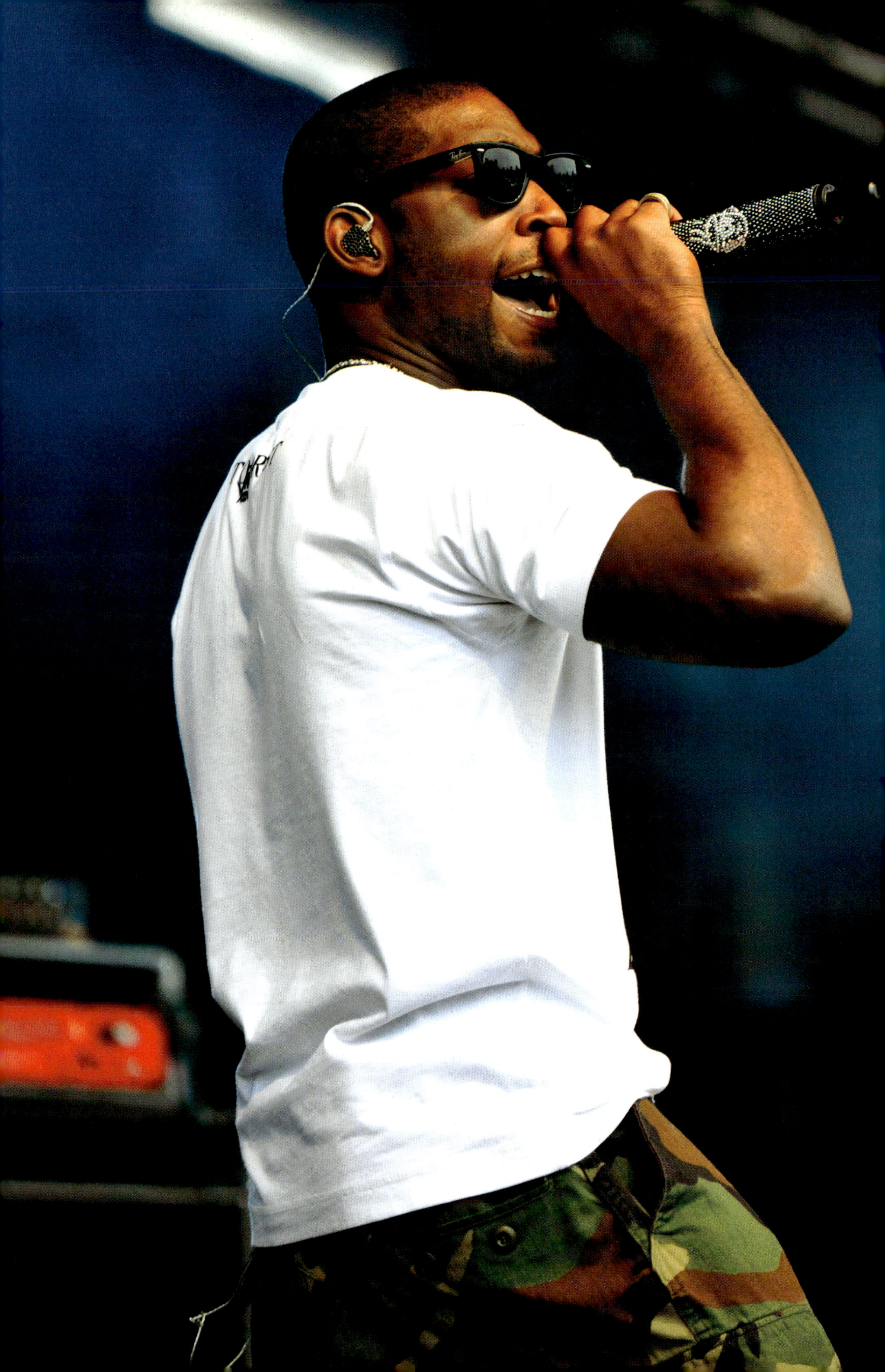

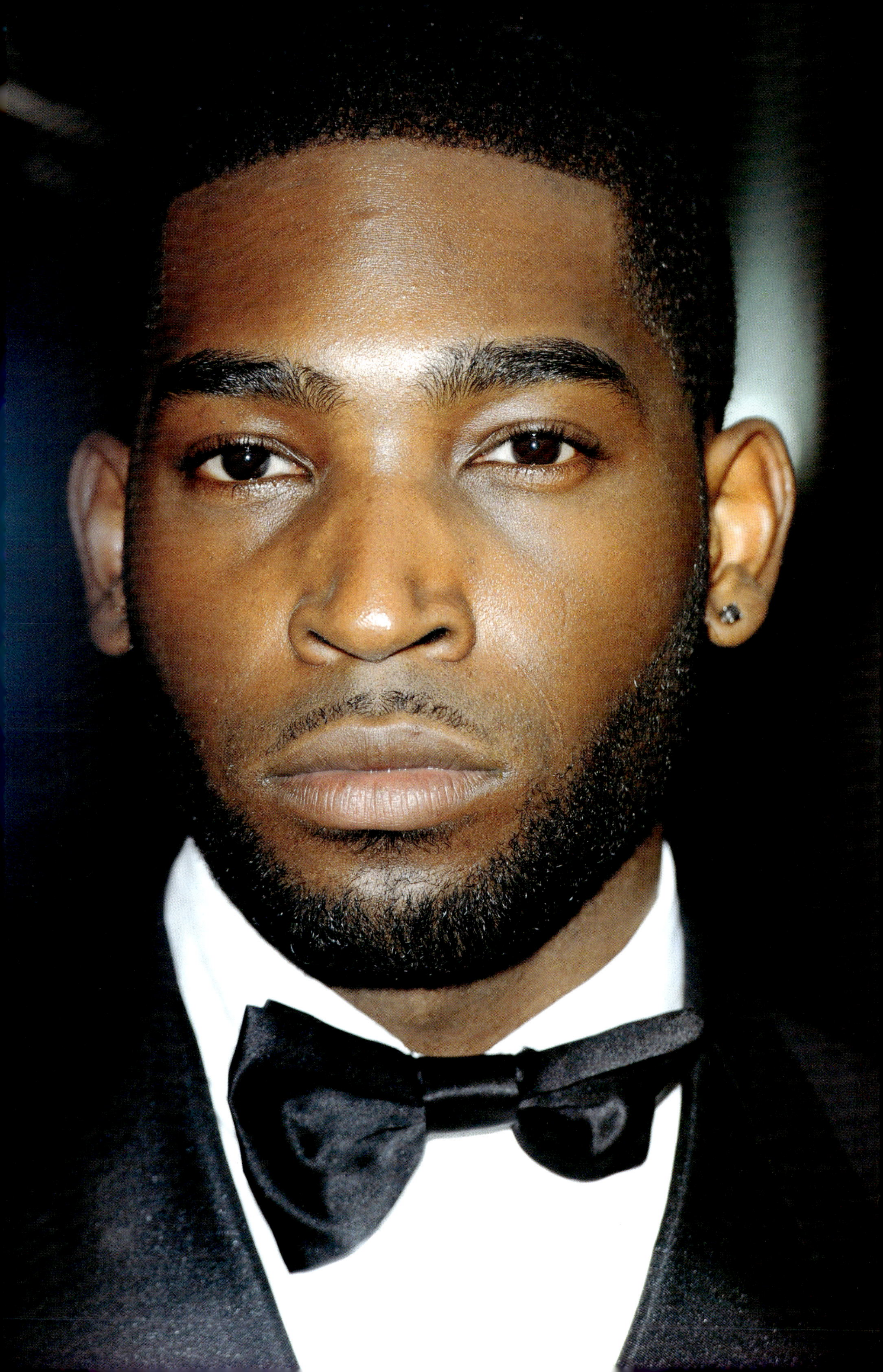

AWARDS

Tinie Tempah is one of the UK's finest new musical talents. This is an opinion not only shared by us, his adoring fans, but also by industry professionals. Tinie has won many awards during his career so far, and there are sure to be plenty more to come. Take a look at some of the best and most prestigious awards that Tinie has won or been nominated for below!

TINIE TEMPAH'S 2010 AWARDS AND NOMINATIONS

MOBO Awards

Nominated:
Best UK Act
Best Song

Won:
Best Newcomer
Best Video - *Frisky*

BT Digital Music Awards

Nominated:
Breakthrough Artist of the Year
Best Male Artist
Best Video - *Frisky*
Best Song - *Frisky*

Won:
Best Newcomer

MTV Europe Music Awards

Nominated:
Best UK and Ireland New Act

2010 Urban Music Awards

Won:
Best Newcomer
Best Hip Hop Act
Best Collaboration for *Pass Out*

Nominated:
Best Video for *Wonderman*

4Music Video Honours

Nominated:
Hottest Boy
Best Video Hook-up for *Frisky* featuring Labrinth

MP3 Music Awards

Won:
The UGG Award (Urban/Garage/Grime)

UK Festival Awards

Won:
Breakthrough Artist

TINIE TEMPAH'S 2011 AWARDS AND NOMINATIONS

South Bank Awards

Nominated:

Pop Music for his album *Disc-Overy*

2011 Brit Awards

Nominated:

Best British Male

Album of the Year

Won:

Best Breakthrough Act

Best Single for *Pass Out*

Ivor Novello Awards

Won:

Best Contemporary Song for *Pass Out*

Something tells us that this is just the beginning of a long line of Awards for Tinnie Tempah, we're sure you'll all agree!

TINIE TEMPAH – CHARITABLE MAN!

Tinie Tempah is not only seriously talented, he's also seriously charitable. He regularly gives up his own time to help out with charity events. Here are just a few of the things Tinie has been involved in for charity. We are sure that there will be many more to come as his career progresses!

Teenage Cancer Trust at the Royal Albert Hall

Tinie Tempah, Jessie J and Maverick Sabre closed the 2011 Concerts for Teenage Cancer Trust with an awesome show. Tinie said, 'Being a teenager can be hard enough at times. But the devastating news that you have cancer is just incomprehensible to me. I have to say that the courage, belief and positivity displayed by these teenagers is astounding and very admirable. It's pretty obvious that what Teenage Cancer Trust does is phenomenal. The help, support and care they give to these young sufferers and their families is amazing and goes a long way in making their lives a lot easier. I can honestly say that I am truly honoured to be part of such a worthy cause.'

Red Cross

Tinie Tempah reportedly donated his pink blazer from the *Frisky* video as one of the donated items to be sold on eBay to benefit the Red Cross relief efforts for Japan.

Transforming A Generation

Tinie Tempah backed Second Chance Week UK, organised by the youth charity Transforming A Generation, which aims to raise awareness of the rehabilitation of young offenders. 'There are a lot of young people out there who feel lost and get into trouble just because they have no direction in their lives,' said the two-time Brit award winner. 'They need a break, and TAG is doing exactly that - giving young people a chance at employment.'

Keep a Child Alive Benefit

Tinie Tempah provided entertainment for the evening at this event, performing his hits alongside Mark Ronson who acted as DJ for the night.

Haiti Fundraiser

Wiley, Tinie Tempah, Sway, MistaJam, The Thirst and Tayo appeared at a fund-raising club night in aid of the Haitian earthquake appeal.

Of course this is just the tip of the iceberg for Tinie's charity work, but it definitely gives us a good idea of just what a great guy he is!

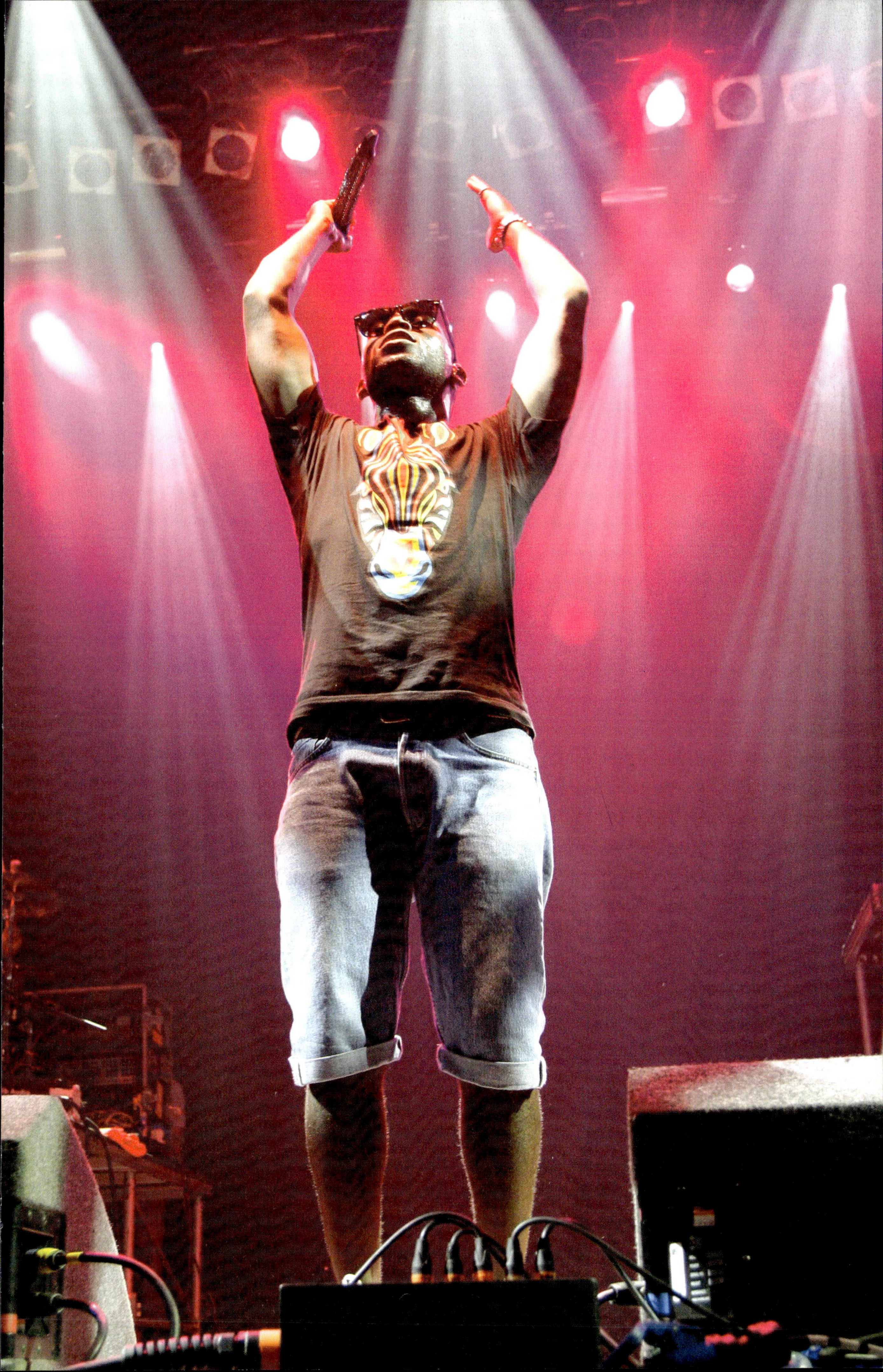

TINIE TEMPAH AND HIS FAMOUS FRIENDS!

Tinie Tempah is friends with some big names in the entertainment scene! Not only has he collaborated with many influential stars but he is also lucky enough to call some of them his friends. Here are just some of the fellow celebs that Tinie has brushed shoulders with during his rise to fame!

Chipmunk – Tinie and Chipmunk toured together in February 2010 and have been firm friends and supporting each other ever since!

Rihanna – Rihanna picked Tinie to tour with her on four dates in the UK. The two got on like a house on fire and consider one another good friends.

The Saturdays – The Saturdays have been snapped at various Tinie Tempah concerts and seem to be big fans of the uber cool rapper!

Ellie Goulding – Ellie sang on Tinie Tempah's popular track *Wonderman* and has nothing but praise for her friend. Speaking to BBC's Newsbeat she said: "He's one of these people I believe in, and not just because of his music, but because he's a lovely person." We couldn't agree more, Ellie!

"It's about not having all that much when you're little and then working very hard and then having a lot more than you used to have and being very grateful," explained Goulding. "So I can relate to it - it's really cool."

Snoop Dogg – Tinie and Snoop Dogg had most of their first correspondence via social networking websites. The two eventually met and performed together and we hear they are still in touch!

Mr Hudson – Tinie always has praise for Mr Hudson. They have worked together several times and are always on hand to support each other both professionally for their music projects and as good friends.

Usher - The two become friends when the *Pass Out* rapper supported him on his European tour. Tinie is a big fan of Usher's choreography on his tours and has a lot of respect for him both as an artist and friend.

Kylie Minogue – Tinie regularly calls up for advice and chats on the phone with the pint sized Australian superstar! He told Australian news website news.com.au, "Kylie's just the coolest chick ever, big sis I call her.

"We're very much friends and she gives me lots of advice. She has told me to always rest as much as possible at any given opportunity, to always eat set meals at set times and keep everything synchronised. Obviously that's not always possible but I look at people like her and she's been doing this for decades and still looks really, really good and remains relevant." He added, "That's a good person to take advice from, I reckon."

TINIE GOSSIP – DID YOU KNOW?

Tinie Tempah is one of the most talked about artists on the hip-hop and rap scene right now. Here are some of the coolest facts, and hottest gossip...

He's a big fan of the Irish boy band The Script, 3OH!3 and Justin Bieber.

Tinie Tempah's name came from him looking through a thesaurus back in year 8 for a catchy stage name to go by, he says 'I was just dazed and that was the time when I really wanted to be an MC. So I looked at all the names like Dizzee Rascal, Tinchy Stryder, and was like "Yea I need a first and a last name!" History was made that day!'

Tiny is not just a pretty face, he was a good student and has 10 GCSEs and 3 A-Levels.

He's the CEO of Disturbing London Records.

It may be hard to believe but Tinie's favourite movie genre is romantic comedies!

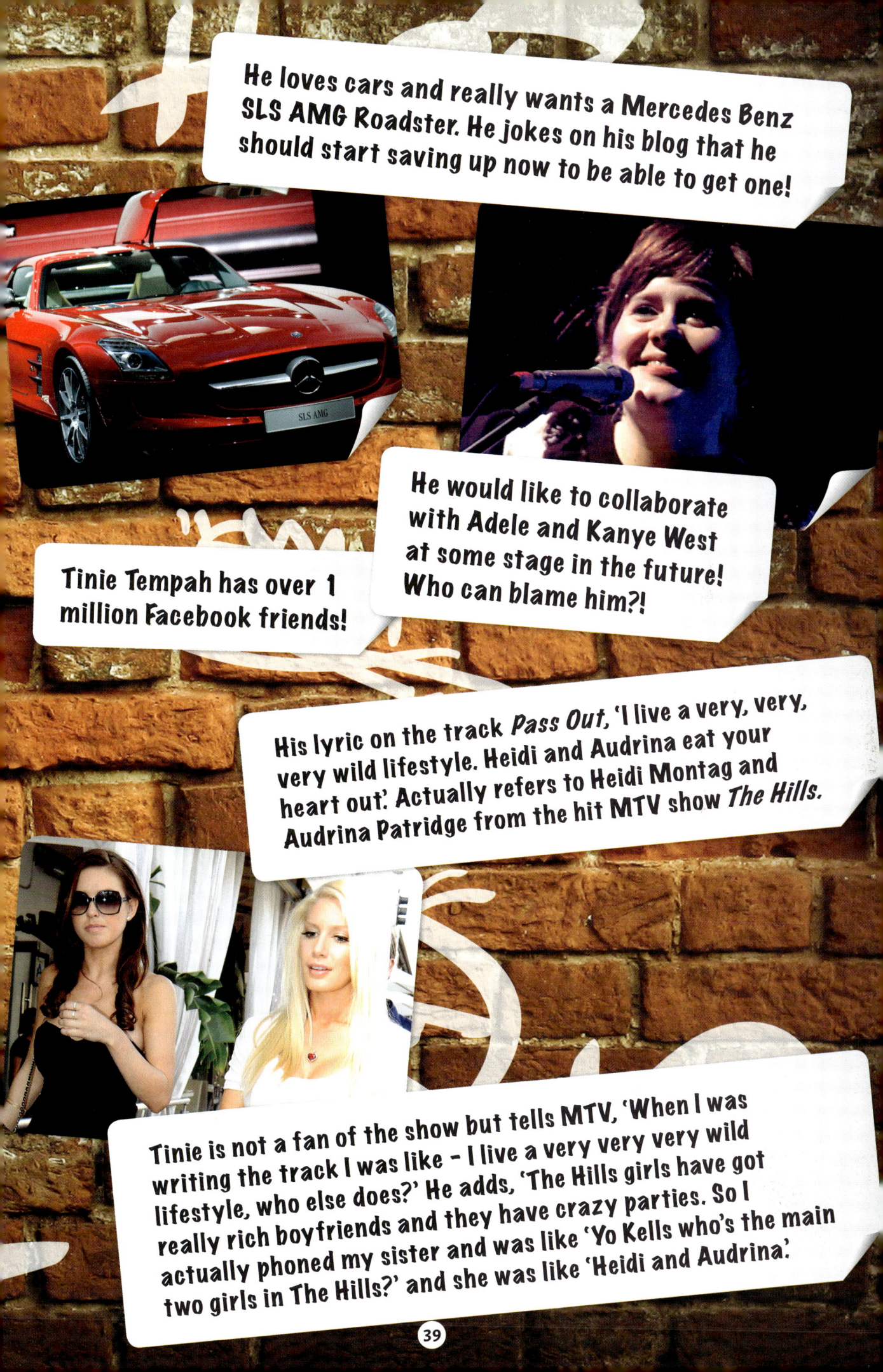

He loves cars and really wants a Mercedes Benz SLS AMG Roadster. He jokes on his blog that he should start saving up now to be able to get one!

He would like to collaborate with Adele and Kanye West at some stage in the future! Who can blame him?!

Tinie Tempah has over 1 million Facebook friends!

His lyric on the track *Pass Out*, 'I live a very, very, very wild lifestyle. Heidi and Audrina eat your heart out'. Actually refers to Heidi Montag and Audrina Patridge from the hit MTV show *The Hills*.

Tinie is not a fan of the show but tells MTV, 'When I was writing the track I was like – I live a very very very wild lifestyle, who else does?' He adds, 'The Hills girls have got really rich boyfriends and they have crazy parties. So I actually phoned my sister and was like 'Yo Kells who's the main two girls in The Hills?' and she was like 'Heidi and Audrina'.

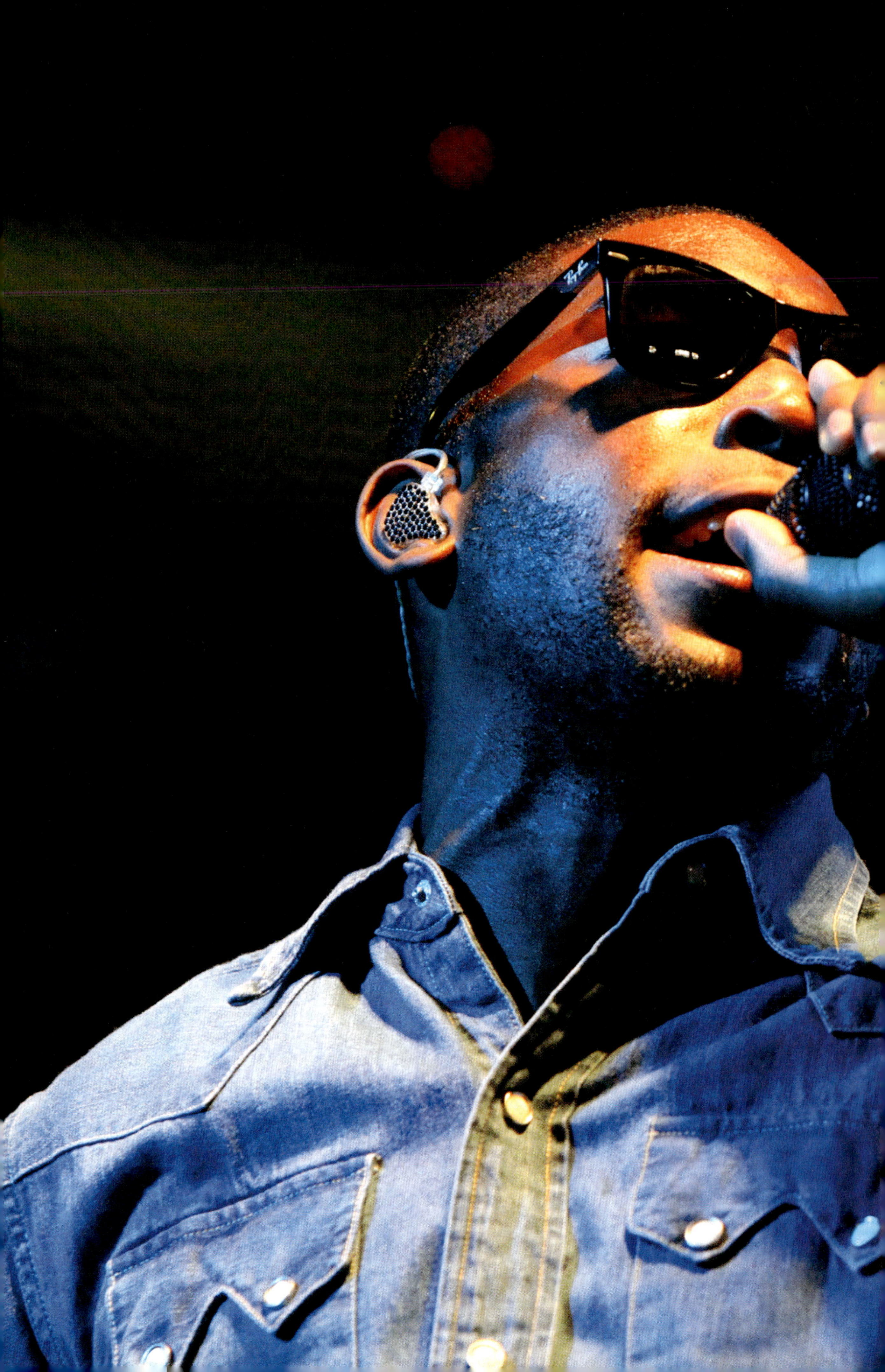

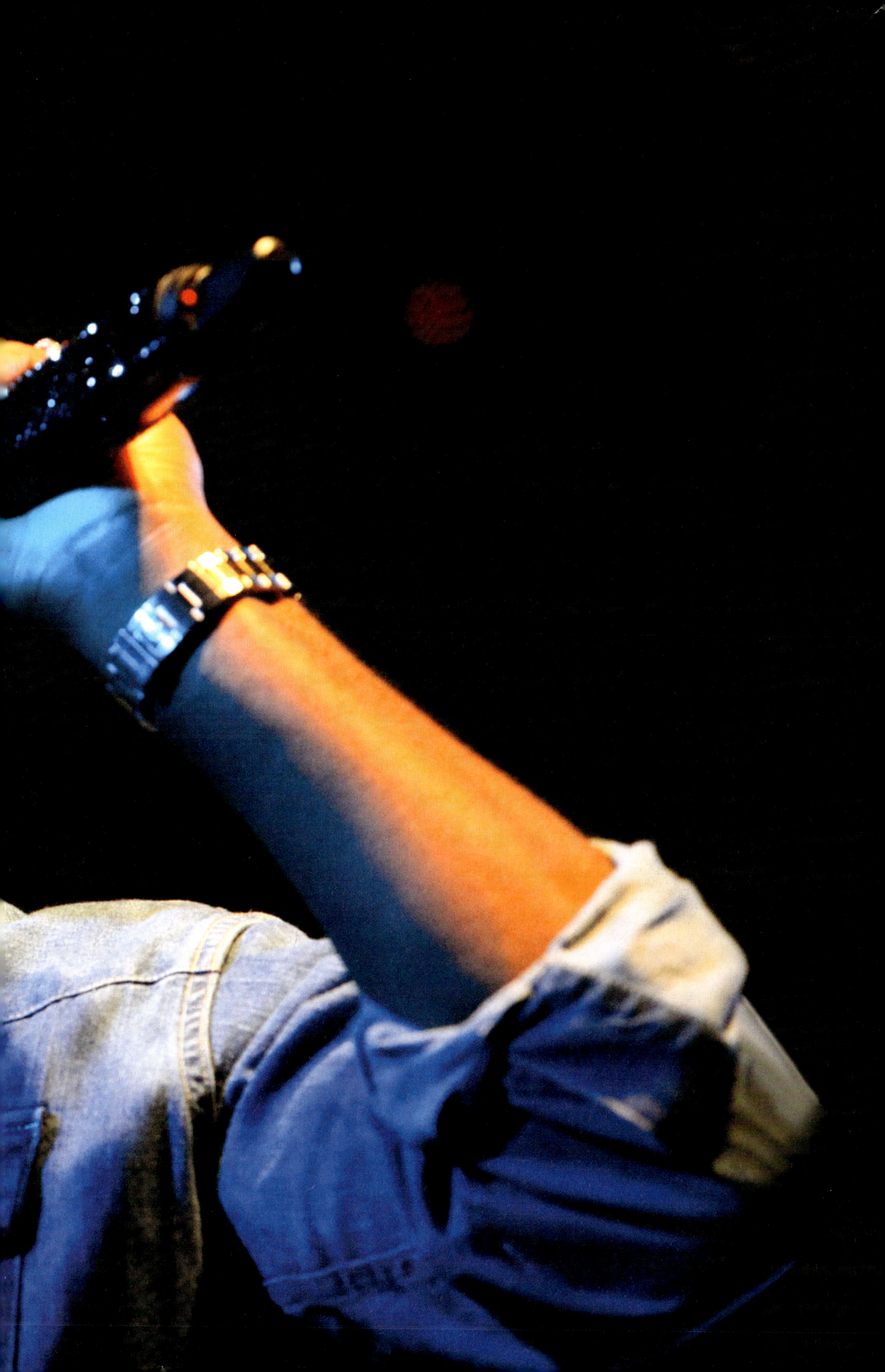

TINIE'S INSPIRATIONS

Tinie is an inspiration to many of his fans. He inspires them to believe that they can do more and become exactly what they want to be. But who inspires Tinie? Who does he draw his inspiration from and why? Let's take a look…

Dizzee Rascal is someone who Tinie really admires and is inspired by his music.

So Solid Crew had a number one hit with *21 Seconds* and Tinie has regularly said that they inspired him to get into music after hearing them on the radio as a teen.

Tinie says that he was influenced by American rappers like Eminem and was inspired by their huge success but also relates to UK stars just as much for different reasons.

Tinie is a big fan of Kylie Minogue, as well as being a good friend! He is impressed by her success and the two get on really well.

Tinie said of Kanye West in a recent interview, "I think he's a very deep individual. I think that if we were in the studio not only would we make something incredible; I believe I would learn a lot from him. I'm very inspired by him so I'd love to make that happen."

About Drake, Tinie says, "He's one of the biggest artists to come out of hip hop in recent times and when you listen to his mixtapes he has mentioned previous UK artists so he seems a bit cultured; I'd definitely like to get in the studio with him."

Believe it or not, Tinie finds Cheryl Cole to be a very inspiring star. When asked if he would like to work with her, he confessed: "I guess I'd have to hear the track. I really admire what she's made of herself from where she's come from." He continued to Metro.co.uk: "She's almost like a British icon and I'm really inspired by that."

Tinie sees Damon Albarn as one of his early inspirations. He loves his dedication to music. Speaking about Damon and Kanye West being inspirational to him, Tinie says, "Whether it's Damon with the Gorillaz - all that animation and the vast amount of band members - or Kanye with the lights, graphics and pyrotechnics. Those two are my inspiration, because they're very relevant in popular culture but also there's a lot more to them. That's definitely the way I would like to be perceived."

He would also like to meet and work with Michael Bublé and Lily Allen so expect some big things from Tinie in the not so distant future!

SO YOU WANNA BE A STAR?

Did you ever dream of reaching the dizzying heights of super-stardom like Tinie Tempah and all of your other famous idols? Well, here are our top tips to help get you started on your way to fortune and fame!

1) Believe in yourself! No-one famous ever got anywhere by thinking the worst of themselves or beating themselves up over their insecurities. Believe that you are special and talented and that you can do whatever you want in life. You might just see that your positive, confident attitude will rub off on others!

2) Know your talents! Decide what it is that you are good at and why. Maybe you are a great singer or rapper, maybe you can play a certain instrument really well? Maybe you are an amazing song writer who lives and breathes to compose your own music and lyrics? Or perhaps you are the next big thing on the dance scene. Whatever your talent or talents may be, recognising them and tuning in to them is a great place to start!

3) Practise, practise, practise! Being a super talented up and coming star like you isn't easy! Take every opportunity to practise your talents in your spare time. Find a good balance between practising your music and keeping up with your school life and friends. Maybe you could involve your friends in your practice time by asking them to help out or be your audience for a while! You never know,

maybe one of them has a talent that you never even knew about that they could practise with you. We all need people around us to help us along the way. Even the biggest of stars like Tinie would agree with that, we're sure!

4) Keep a journal! Try keeping a journal or a notebook handy so that when you have a new idea, a thought or a sudden burst of musical inspiration you can jot it down. You will find this a great place to write lyrics or notes and keep everything safely together. When you are lacking inspiration take a peek at your journal and the notes, pictures and lyrics you have written down and maybe they will help!

5) Challenge yourself! Keep challenging yourself to do new things in your chosen area of talent. If you are a singer or a rapper, try different styles of songs that you have never explored before and see where they take you. Don't be scared of stepping out of your comfort zone and performing things that might not always seem like the obvious choice. You might just find that you surprise yourself along the way!

Last of all, but probably most importantly:

6) Have FUN! Once you stop enjoying what you are doing, then it can start to feel like a chore rather than having fun and doing something that you love. Keep yourself inspired and remember that half the fun of dreaming of being famous is the things you experience along the way!

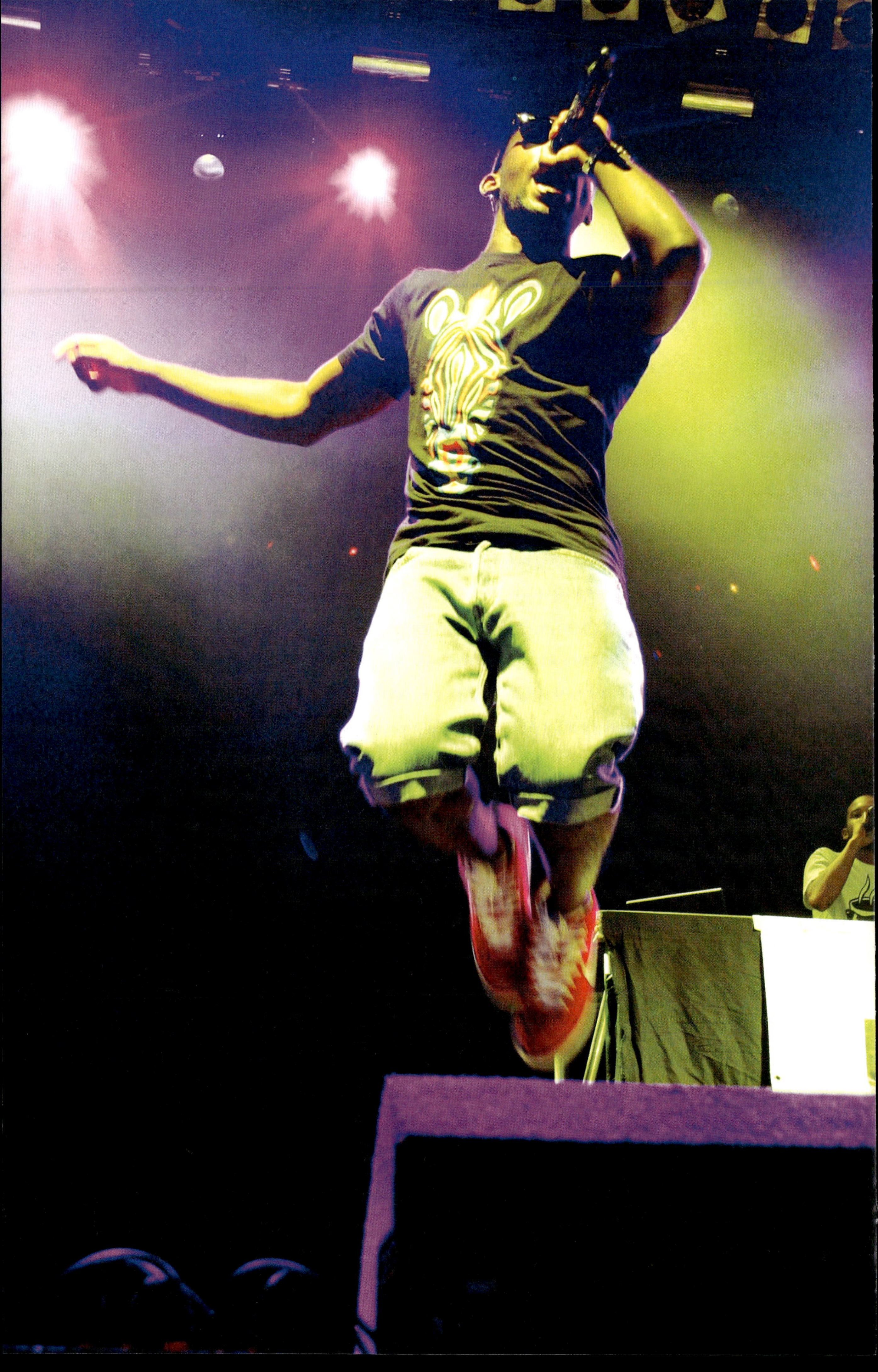

COLOURING IN

47

COLLABORATIONS

Tinie Tempah has proved that he can well and truly hold his own in the music world with the release of his album and some amazing tracks but he has also collaborated with some of music's top talent along the way. Check out who Tinie Tempah has collaborated with and what they worked on together!

Who: Ellie Goulding – British singer-songwriter with a great fan base.

What: Tinie and Ellie Goulding worked together on the track *Wonderman*.

When: 4th October 2010 on the *Disc-Overy* album.

Who: Eric Turner - American singer-songwriter who is currently living in Sweden. He is the lead singer in the band Street Fighting Man and is also a teacher.

What: Tinie and Eric worked together on the track *Written in the Stars*.

When: 27th September 2010 on the *Disc-Overy* album.

Who: Range – American singer, songwriter and producer.

What: Tinie and Range worked together on the track *Just a Little*.

When: 4th October 2010. Features on the *Disc-Overy* album.

Who: Labrinth – English singer-songwriter and successful record producer.

What: Tinie and Labrinth worked together on the tracks *Frisky* and *Pass Out*.

When: *Frisky* was released on 7th June 2010. *Pass Out* was released on 28th February 2010.

Who: Emeli Sandé – A singer-songwriter from Scotland.

What: Tinie and Emeli Sandé worked together on the track *Let Go*.

When: 4th October 2010 on the *Disc-Overy* album.

Who: Swedish House Mafia – A Swedish house music group.

What: Tinie worked with Swedish House Mafia on the track *Miami 2 Ibiza*.

When: Released 4th October 2010 and features on the *Disc-Overy* album.

Who: Kelly Rowland – Successful American singer and ex 'Destiny's Child' band member.

What: Tinie and Kelly Rowland worked together on the track *Invincible*.

When: The fourth official track from *Disc-Overy* released on 26th December 2010.

LYRICS QUIZ

Tinie Tempah comes up with some great tracks which are known worldwide, but can you tell which one of these quotes is NOT a classic Tinie Tempah lyric? Pick the odd one out.

1. Would you risk it for a chocolate biscuit?
   Would you risk it for a chocolate biscuit?
   Yeah, I'm suspicious, she looks delicious,
   She likes to talk a lot, that's why I call her Trisha,
   Her nails are manicured, her hair has been conditioned.

2. I see the bright lights shine in your face,
   I'm counting on you to take it all away,
   I saw the chosen one,
   They're calling your name.

3. I used to listen to you, don't wanna bring arms house
   I got so many clothes, I keeps some in my aunt's house.

4. Turning around and around, feel like my feet won't touch the ground.
   I was lost but now I'm found and my heart won't make a sound.

5. Scene one. Everybody get in your positions.
   Pay attention, and listen.
   We're tryna get this all in one take, so let's try and make that happen.
   Take one...Action!!!

COLOURING IN

Tinie Tempah
Look To

Tinie Tempah is already more successful than most UK artists. He has achieved dizzying heights in a relatively short period of time, so can you imagine what things might be like for him in a few years time? Let's take a look to the future and imagine what Tinie Tempah's career might be like a few years from now with some mock newspaper headlines which are, of course, totally made up for now, but definitely possible in the long term. See some fun predictions below!

"TINIE STORMS THE STATES!"

Tinie has spoken of his desire to conquer the American music scene. Perhaps he will do this in the next couple of years. With famous friends like Usher who know the American music scene well, he is sure to be given a helping hand along the way. His persistence and determination will surely lead him along this path soon! A sell out tour in the US would be a dream come true for our ambitious star.

"TINIE DESIGNS HIS OWN FOOTWEAR RANGE!"

We all know that Tinie Tempah is fashion and footwear obsessed. It is possible that not too long from now, he will have his own personal range of designs ranging from footwear to glasses and other trade-mark 'Tinie' clothing and accessory favourites!

Future Edition 2012

The Future

Turn to page 6

"TINIE RAISES MILLIONS FOR CHARITY!"

Tinie already does his bit for various charities. Always willing to help out and get involved in projects to help those in need. Who knows though, maybe in years to come Tinie will be fundraising and donating millions of his own earnings to charities and worthwhile causes.

"SHOCK COLLABORATIONS FOR TINIE TEMPAH!"

Maybe Tinie Tempah will shock us down the line with his next collaborations. Perhaps he will work with people that we wouldn't generally pair his music with and maybe it will turn out to be a ground-breaking musical experience! We already know that Tinie is good friends with the very talented Kylie Minogue, so maybe something along these lines might just happen. Who knows!

"UK RAPPER FINDS L-O-V-E"

Tinie has been associated with various different female celebrities and girlfriends but he's not anywhere near settling down, preferring instead to focus on his work. We wonder who the lucky lady will be when he does eventually decide to settle down. Will she be famous, a fellow musician maybe? Or perhaps she will be someone completely out of the music and celebrity scene. Time will tell….

Of course, these things may never actually happen, but we can't wait to find out what the future has in store for Tinie Tempah. We imagine only good things for this hugely talented star though, that's for sure!

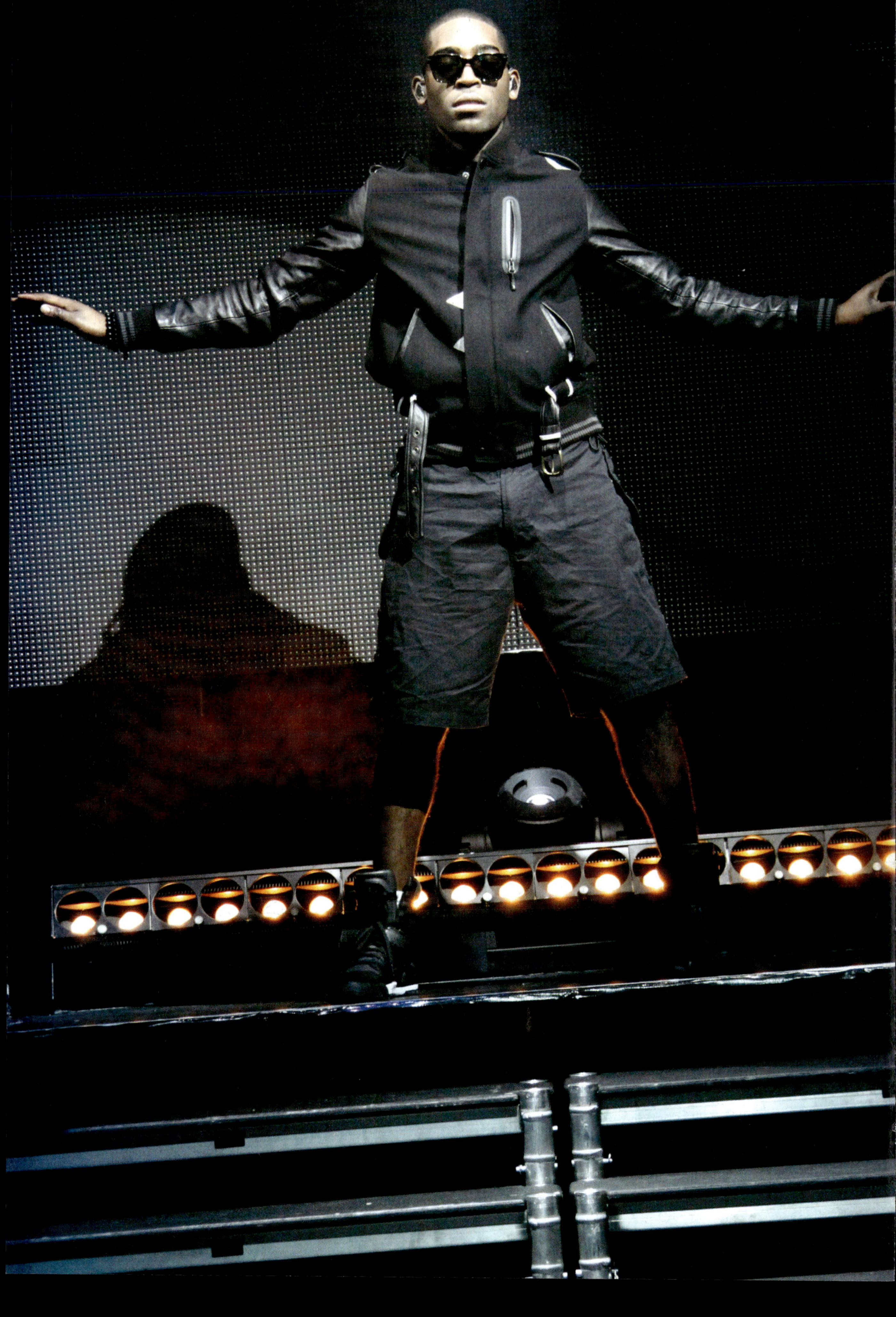

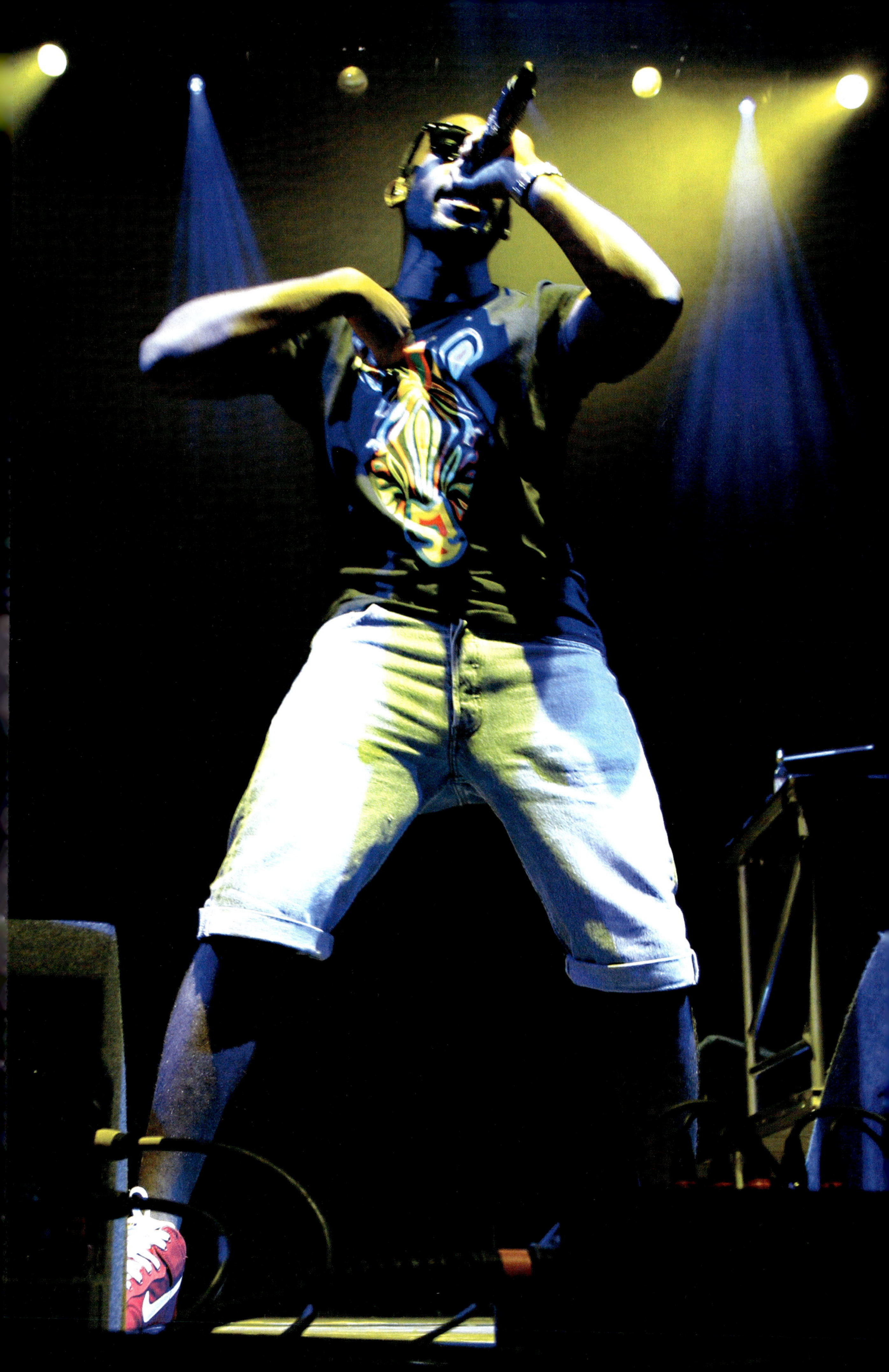

TINIE FASHION FOCUS!

Tinie Tempah is about as fashionable as they come! He is stylish, but in his own unique way and is famous for not following the standard rules of fashion in what he wears. He loves to look good and takes pride in his appearance which all just adds to his charm and appeal.

One of the stand out accessories in Tinie Tempah's eye catching style has to be those amazing Ray-Ban Wayfarer glasses that he always wears. We think that they have become almost like a trade mark fashion piece and something that his fans always associate him with. They look great and always add to that final, polished 'Tinie' look.

Tinie wears a very mixed selection of clothing to achieve his stylish look, but he is often spotted wearing a lot of denim, both on his jackets and baggy jeans.

Tinie is a huge fan of art and loves bright and exciting colours. He can often be seen wearing black with a splash of colour on artistic t-shirts and shirts with vibrant patterns and designs. He loves to stay current and his style draws upon inspiration from both the world of art and the rap and hip-hop scene.

One of Tinie's big fashion loves are his trainers. He loves to wear a great variety of styles and appreciates those with a retro twist and an 80's feel to them. He often blogs about styles which have caught his eye and he is a big fan of Nike Hi-Tops, Air Max and Converse. The bolder and the brighter the better for Tinie, who just hates to blend into the background!

With plenty of attitude and a defined sense of personality in all that he wears, Tinie is one of the best dressed musicians in the spotlight this year. Ultimately he knows what he likes and what works well for him and he wears it with confidence, now that's the key to looking great!

A-Z OF TINIE

There are so many words to describe Tinie Tempah. He is such a unique and talented star that we think he deserves his own A-Z. Check out the A-Z of Tinie Tempah. Maybe you can come up with some of your own?

A is for Artistic. Tinie is artistic in his approach to music and for his love of art in fashion.

B is for Brainy! He is well educated and plans to return to study at University at some stage.

C is for Charming. Tinie is definitely a charmer. He knows how to flatter, impress and sweep us off our feet.

D is for Daring! Tinie Tempah dares to believe in himself and in his music. He takes chances with the songs he releases and mixes different genres that wouldn't always be everyone's first choice.

E is for Engaging. When Tinie talks, people listen. He always gets his point across in interviews and live on stage.

F is for Fans! Tinie loves his fans and always makes time for them and appreciates their support.

G is for Girls. Tinie has confessed to being a 'sucker for a pretty face' and likes to socialise and date!

H is for Happy! Tinie Tempah is in a great place in his career right now and is happy and content with how well things are going.

I is for Impressive. Tinie always impresses fans and industry professionals with his music and his attitude towards the music he brings to the table.

J is for Joker! Tinie has a great sense of humour and knows how to take a joke. He doesn't take himself too seriously.

K is for Kind. Tinie is kind-hearted and cool!

L is for Loving. Tinie Tempah loves his family, friends and fans.

M is for Movie fan. Tinie loves movies, especially romantic comedies.

N is for Nominations. Tinie has been nominated for and won various different awards in the music industry, making him very well respected!

O is for Original! We love Tinie for his sense of originality.

P is for Picky! He likes to pick and choose with his clothing, favouring certain brands and styles.

Q is for Quick learner! Tinie Tempah has been a quick learner in the music industry. He has quickly picked up the basic tricks of the trade and is now well on his way to super stardom!

R is for Relevant. He uses the internet, his websites and blogs to create relevant content that his fans want to read about.

S is for Stylish! Tinie is a well-dressed guy! He likes nothing better than treating himself to the latest clothes and shoes.

T is for Trendy. If it's hot and on trend, you can guarantee Tinie knows about it!

U is for Unique. Because Tinie really is one in a million!

V is for Very good looking. He cares about his appearance, but isn't vain.

W is for Writing great lyrics. Tinie has the ability to write relevant and topical lyrics.

X is for X'Citing! Okay we had to cheat slightly there, but we think Tinie is truly an exciting new talent and will go very far.

Y is for Young! Tinie is only at the beginning of his career as he joined the industry from a young age. This means he will be around for years to come, bringing us exciting new music!

Z is for Zany – He likes to embrace his slightly zany personality and expresses this in different ways through his music and fashion sense.

ANSWERS

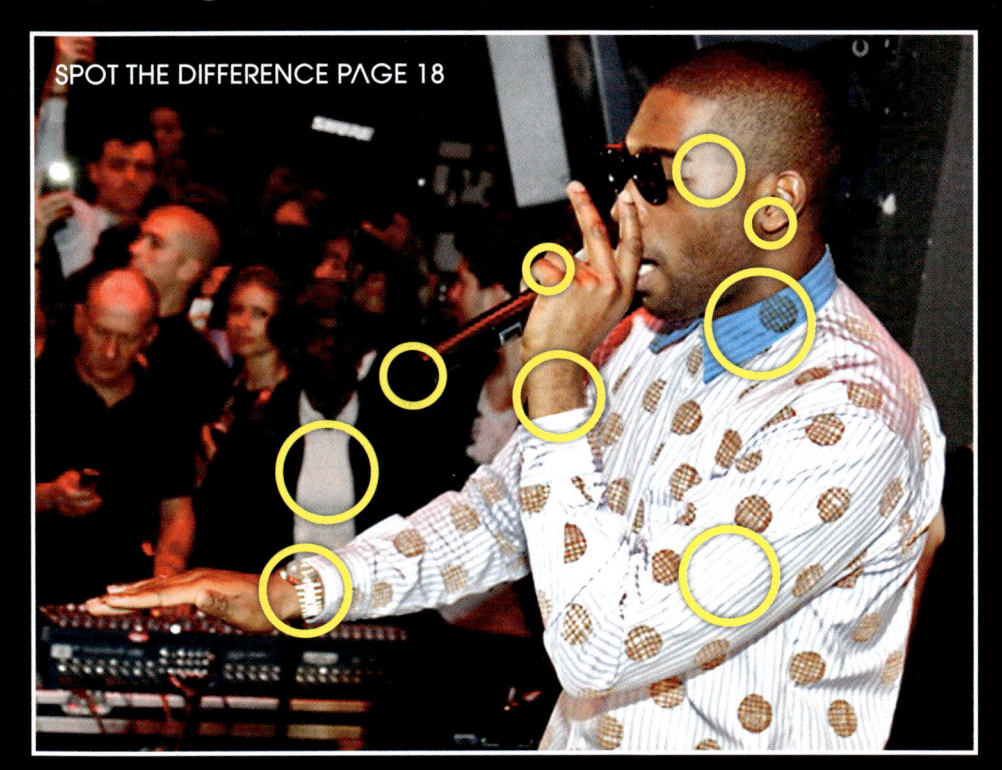

SPOT THE DIFFERENCE PAGE 18

WORDSERCH PAGE 19

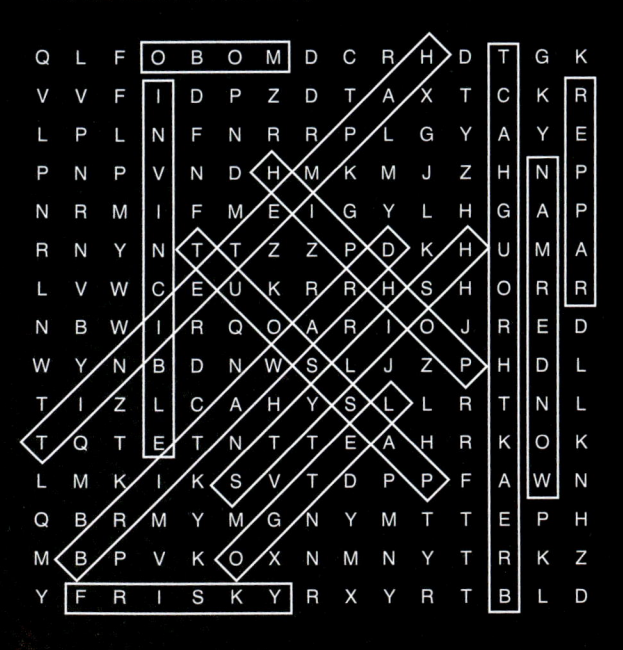

CROSSWORD PAGE 27

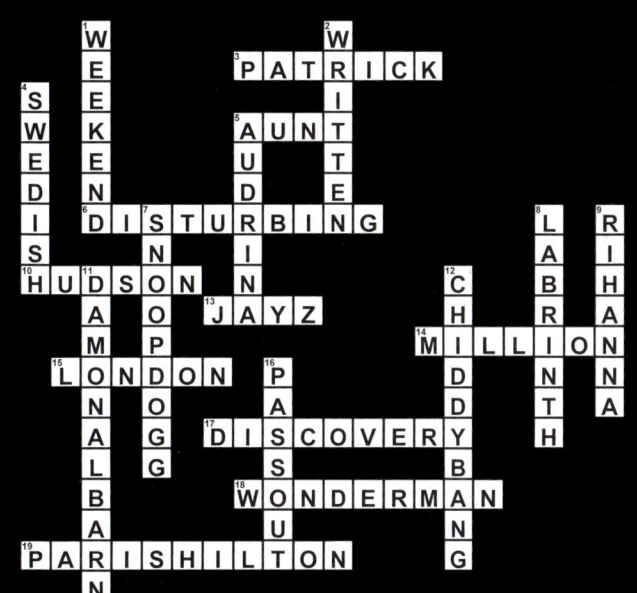

LYRICS QUIZ PAGE 50. ANSWER IS NO. 4.

WHERE'S TINIE?